In the p

All the kids are in the park. It is the big kids, Sam and Asher, against Nat, Dan and Meg.

Dad is the referee. Nan and Pop get the best spot to see.

Sam kicks to Asher. Asher runs in but Dan is too quick. Dan kicks high in the air.

Now Meg is there. She gets a goal. She runs with her hands in the air.

Miss Good trots down from her flat. She stops next to Nan.

Miss Good looks at the kids and squints. She tells Nan, "I lost my specs and I cannot see a thing!"

Asher gets the next goal.

Pam swoops into the goal.
POP!
"That is a red card for Pam!" yells Dad.

Just then, Gus bursts out on to the park. He has Mum's sunhat. He runs off!

All the kids run to get Gus. Sam grabs Gus and Nat grabs the sunhat.

Mack, Meg's rabbit, is next to the oak tree. He is munching on the weeds.

Meg picks up Mack and pats his soft fur.

Mum turns up in her van with Miss Toil. They have been at the market. They have loads of muffins left!

Mum and Miss Toil hand out the muffins. All the kids dig in.

In the park   Level 5: Story 50

Words to blend

market	high	goal
Good	such	thing
looks	swoops	oak
tree	munching	weeds
been	loads	sunhat
hand	next	rabbit

In the park

Level 5: Story 50

Before reading

Synopsis: The children have fun in the park – playing football, having fun with their pets and eating muffins.

Review phoneme/s: ar or ur ow oi ear air ure er

Story discussion: Look at the cover, and read the title together. Ask: *Who can you see on the cover? What are they doing in the park?* Share ideas about what might happen in the story.

Link to prior learning: Remind children of the graphemes they have been learning in Level 5. Display the graphemes *ar, or, ur, ow, oi, ear, air, ure* and *er*. How quickly can children read each grapheme? Ask them to say and write a word that includes each grapheme.

Vocabulary check: Swoops – rushes down towards something. Can children use their hands to demonstrate a swooping motion?

Decoding practice: Display words using the focus graphemes (you could use children's suggestions from the Link to prior learning activity). Ask children to add the dots under single-letter graphemes and dashes under digraphs and trigraphs. Ask them to sound out and blend each word.

Tricky word practice: Display the word *have*. Ask children to circle the tricky part (e, which is silent). Encourage children to practise writing and reading this word.

After reading

Apply learning: Discuss the story. Ask: *How are all the characters feeling at the end of the story? Why? Do you think this makes a good ending to the story?*

Comprehension

- Which two characters score a goal?
- What has happened to Mum's sunhat?
- What snack do Mum and Miss Toil bring to the park?

Fluency

- Pick a page that most of the group read quite easily. Ask them to reread it with pace and expression. Model how to do this if necessary.
- Turn to pages 6–7, and ask children to read the words Miss Good says. Can they read with lots of expression so that it sounds as if she is really talking?
- Practise reading the words on page 17.

In the park   **Level 5: Story 50**

Tricky words review

all	do	are
so	there	you
have	your	she
oh	me	said
they	out	one